MW01097643

Criminal Psychology
The Criminal Mind of a
Serial Killer

By Shawn Becker

© **Copyright by Shawn Becker 2016 - All rights reserved.**

The contents of this book may not be reproduced, duplicated or transmitted without direct written permission from the author.

Under no circumstances will any legal responsibility or blame be held against the publisher for any reparation, damages, or monetary loss due to the information herein, either directly or indirectly.

Legal Notice:

This book is copyright protected. This is only for personal use. You cannot amend, distribute, sell, use, quote or paraphrase any part or the content within this book without the consent of the author.

Disclaimer Notice:

Please note the information contained within this document is for educational and entertainment purposes only. Every attempt has been made to provide accurate, up to date and reliable complete information. No warranties of any kind are expressed or implied. Readers acknowledge that the author is not engaging in the rendering of legal, financial, medical or professional advice. The content of this book has been derived from various sources. Please consult a licensed professional before attempting any techniques outlined in this book.

By reading this document, the reader agrees that under no circumstances are is the author responsible for any losses, direct or indirect, which are incurred as a result of the use of information contained within this document, including, but not limited to, — errors, omissions, or inaccuracies.

Table of Contents

Introduction

To the untrained eye, a serial killer looks just like any other member of the public. They wear the same clothes, they eat the same food and they go about their daily lives, as any normal person would do. But there is a difference in them, which is unquantifiable; it is the deadly secret that all serial killers hide from the outside world.

If they weren't able to conceal this secret so well, many cold-blooded killings could have been prevented. So if we could see deep within their souls and spot the things that made them the way they are, maybe we could stop them from becoming serial killers in the first place.

With this book, I aim to get inside the mind of a serial killer, to show what makes them tick and to see if there are any personality traits that are the same across the wide range of different serial killers there have been through time.

Finally, I will take a look at the top 5 serial killer personalities and 10 of the most famous serial killers in history. This will give us an insight into the mind of a serial killer and a better understanding of the things that turn people into cold and calculating killing machines...

Chapter 1: What Turns a Person into a Serial Killer?

What is a serial killer? A serial killer is someone who kills at least three people over the course of at least one month with a significant break between each murder. The FBI will consider 2 or more murders to be serial killings, each one committed separately while other authorities may consider 4 murders to be the start of a serial killing spree. The one thing we must not do is confuse a serial killer with a mass murderer or a spree killer, terms that are often used interchangeably but all of which are different. A mass murderer will kill a number of people in one single incident, while a spree killer will commit a number of murders in at least two locations in a very short period of time. On the other hand, we have the serial spree killer, a person who commits sequential murders over periods of time extending to weeks or months but without the "cooling off period" we associate with a serial killer.

Most, if not all serial killers exhibit some or all of these common traits:

1. Abuse of Alcohol or Other Substances

Many people who go on to become serial killers are exposed to substance and/or alcohol abuse while still in the womb. This causes several very serious defects present at birth, including retardation, issues with the central nervous system, smaller eye openings and a smaller head and brain, should the baby survive beyond birth.

Even worse are those who grow up in homes where others expose them to substance abuse. This can cause conditions such as attachment disorders, ADHD, feelings of inadequacy, self-doubt, depression, and some behavioral problems. These will be evident from a young age and, according to statistics from the FBI, more than 70%[1] of known serial killers lived in a home where substance abuse was the norm and caused severe problems. That said, very few serial killers have ever been found to be addicted to any substance or alcohol, perhaps a reaction to their upbringing.

2. Childhood Psychological Abuse

In reality, it should go without saying that almost all serial killers suffered some kind of abuse as a child. Information gathered from numerous interviews with known serial

---

[1] Stone, Michael H., M.D. 2009. "*The Anatomy of Evil*". Amherst, NY: Prometheus Books.

killers, have shown that two of the main forms of abuse, were neglect and emotional abuse. They would suffer from constant humiliation and the discipline that was meted out to them was very often unpredictable, wicked, destructive, and very unfair. Even simple neglect can cause massive problems in terms of development, or lack of it and the child is likely to become desensitized, believing that a world without emotion is normal. As such he or she is liable to grow up feeling no empathy for anyone else.

Emotional abuse will impair their self-esteem and it will interfere with their ability to be able to function normally in society, affect their chances of succeeding in terms of academics and will render them unable to or finding it difficult to form healthy relationships, in particular, intimate ones. This is why we often hear that a serial killer has had many jobs, failing to hold on to anyone for any period and that they rarely have loving relationships with anyone. Although this is not always the case, as you will find out later in this book. There have been several cases of serial killers being in relationships and at the same time being cold-blooded murderers.

3. Violent Sexual Events in Childhood

There is some material that is accessible that reveals the effects that violent sexual events in childhood can have adverse effects on development. Several male serial killers are known to have been made to dress up in female clothing as a way of being punished. And those who were made to watch serious sexual acts between members of the family or parents suffered some of the worst effects. On top of that, some were strongly punished when caught masturbating and others were the victims of sexual abuse, usually by a parent or other member of the family. Childhood experiences such as these will often cause a person to create violent and vivid fantasies that they carry through to adulthood.

Suffering abuse as a child can often lead to feelings of isolation, especially socially, seizures, issues with self-control and learning difficulties. Many serial killers did for example not complete their high school years. Children that get abused can also develop a feeling of powerlessness over themselves and their body. As you will read further inside this book many serial killers have an affinity to power. Their childhood experiences of powerlessness can probably be big reasons for this affinity.

All of the research that has been done into the link between childhood abuse and serial killing leads to one compelling conclusion – serial killers are not born; **they are made**.

4. Wetting the Bed

This is by no means a definite and, on its own bed-wetting is no longer credited to being a predictor of violent tendencies later on. However, there is speculation that it could be related to animal cruelty and to arson. Why? Researchers[2] say that those who persistently wet the bed after reaching the age of 5 feel demeaned, in particular when parents or other authority figures belittle or tease them. As a reaction, the child may then go on to set fires or abuse animals as a way of venting their frustration or anger.

In 2004 Shirley Lynn Scott wrote an article "What Makes Serial Killers Tick?" that states that "... 60% of multiple murderers wet their beds past adolescence. Kenneth Bianchi apparently spent many a night marinating in urine-soaked sheets." This number should, however, be taken with a grain of salt.

In the seventies, Kenneth Bianchi and his cousin Angelo Buono committed the known "Hillside Strangler murders". They presented themselves as undercover police officers as a way to lure women into their car only to kidnap, rape and then strangle them to death.

---

[2] Singer, Stephen D.; Hensley, Christopher 2004. "Learning theory to childhood and adolescent fire setting: Can it lead to serial murder?".

5. Growing up Isolated and Lonely

When you look back at the families of serial killers, you can clearly see that they were not in tune, were deeply at odds with one another. They cannot have a relationship that doesn't malfunction and that doesn't debilitate them in some way and you will also notice that these families move to new homes on a regular basis and the children very often wind up in a shelter before they reach the age of 18.

What it comes down to is the fact that these children are never provided with a stable loving home as they grow up, there is no stability in their young lives at all. Because of this, they end up being unable to make their own relationships and become loners. If you look into the background of some of the serial killers, you will see one thing that resonates throughout all of them – their classmates could never remember them and they never had close school friends. In fact, they would frequently be bullied and, because of this, would develop anti-social behavior and tendencies at a young age. Look carefully and you will see these young people start to dabble in theft and arson, display aggression and hostility, develop a fascination with dangerous weapons and will have no regard for the rights of any other person.

6. Fantasies

Everyone has fantasies at some time in their life but, for most of us, these fantasies are out of reach and are something we never strive to achieve. The serial killer will fantasize about violation and control. Research has shown that few serial killers ever had positive fantasies when they were growing up, instead, their fantasies would revolve around mutilation, of themselves and others, including their own genitals and are mostly violent and aggressive.

A serial killer in the making will never talk to anyone about these fantasies and thoughts but they will find that the thoughts begin to occur with terrifying frequency. Before they commit their very first murder, the fantasies will be focused on that murder. After that, they will fantasize about each successive murder, how to make it more successful and more efficient.

7. A Preference for Auto-Eroticism

Many serial killers avoided social events and parties as a child. They never went through the sexual experimentation stage that many young teenagers go through today, preferring auto-erotic activities instead, such as pornographic material and masturbation. In some cases, the masturbation would be obsessive, as it was with Andrei Chikatilo, a Soviet serial killer responsible for the sexual assault, mutilation, and murder of more than 50 people. His penis was heavily scarred because of the aggressive nature of his masturbation.

The serial killer tends not to have any real social structure to his or her life and is therefore not able to have a normal sexual relationship. Because of this, they feel forced into undertaking solo activities. It isn't just pornographic magazines or books that fuel their sexual fantasies, detective magazines will often go into lurid detail about the sexual nature of a murder, thus providing both arousal and a link between murder and sex.

8. Moving on to Fetishism and Voyeurism in Adulthood

Many serial killers exhibit an interest in fetishism and voyeurism from a young age. They will typically start off with reasonably harmless activity, such as becoming peeping toms but many will then move on to breaking and entering, and rape, followed by murder. Because dominance and bondage feature so highly in many of the more dangerous sexual activities, it is no surprise that many serial killers take this route once they reach adolescence.

9. Violent Fantasies on Animals

Most serial killers, that have been interviewed, confess that they acted out some of their more violent fantasies on animals before moving on to human victims. Because many serial killers come from a dysfunctional background, this type of behavior tends to be ignored or not seen at all. One famous example of this was Jeffrey Dahmer, whose father didn't see anything wrong with his son spending a lot of time dissecting animals. Acts such as this cause great amounts of pleasure to the young killers and they use the animals to perfect their art before they try it out on a human victim.

10. Physical Injuries

It has been suggested that there is a strong link between head trauma and violent/ aggressive behavior. Physical abuse, accidents and brain trauma caused by birth are some examples of what could have caused these traumas. Damage to the hypothalamus, temporal lobe or limbic brain can result in spontaneous aggression and this is because these three areas of the brain are related to motivation, emotion, aggression, and hormones. Injuries to these areas can also result in some forms of amnesia and seizures. There is also some research to indicate that the pre-frontal cortex, which is the area of the brain related to judgment and planning, does not function as it should in a psychopath.

There have been numerous serial killers who suffered head injuries. David Berkowitz, Kenneth Bianchi, John Gacy and Leonard Lake are all serial killers that suffered from some kind of head injury or disease. Together these men have stabbed, shot, raped and strangled more than 50 people.

Chapter 2: Nature or Nurture? An In-depth Look at the Mind and Makeup of a Serial Killer

Did you ever wonder what went through the mind of Jeffery Dahmer, one of the most infamous serial killers in history? Let me try to give you an idea of how he killed. A young man lies unconscious before him as Dahmer drills into his head and pours sulfuric acid in. He has a fantasy, to create a zombie. Within 24 hours the man is dead. Dahmer removes his head and mummifies it, putting it in the freezer with skulls of previous victims. Next, he cuts up the rest of the body and puts the blood, skin, and bone into a large container of acid to dissolve it. Throughout all of this, Dahmer showed no anger. He did not do it for revenge nor did he do it for financial gain. He did it because he wanted to, because of desire and because of impulse.

Criminal psychologists, from all over the world, have studied killers like Dahmer, trying to work out why they do it, how they became so violent. They came up with two different schools of thought:

- Are these killers born with genes that determine who and what they will become?
- Or is it something that happened to them as a child?

While it is important that we understand how these people turn into serial killers, it is even more important to determine exactly what it is that defines a serial killer and why they are so different from other murderers.

One of the biggest things that separate the serial killer from any other type of killer is the motive they have to kill. A "normal" murder could be down to anything from a family dispute to gang violence, from financial issues to a dispute between friends. A murderer has some kind of revenge to carry out, something personal against a certain person. A serial killer doesn't have that – they are driven purely by instinct, by that desire to kill. Because of this, serial killers will often kill strangers.

According to the criminal profiler, Grover Goodwin, after collecting data from more than 100 serial killers and their more than 700 victims, almost 90% of victims were strangers; 1% were family and 3% were friends. This goes some way towards explaining how the serial killer gets away with murder for so long – there simply isn't anything to tie the victims together and nothing that links them to the killer.

Movies have gone a long way towards idealizing serial killers in our minds. The character of Hannibal Lector, for example, is an example of an intelligent man who works in riddles, a man with an incredibly high IQ – most of our serial killers don't get an education that goes past high school. In fact, out of the killers that Goodwin studies, just 16% went to college and only 4% of those graduated. However, despite the apparent lack of education, a serial killer must display the wit and the cleverness needed to be able to murder multiple victims and to dispose of the bodies without being caught and without leaving any real evidence.

Sadly, movies have also put images into our minds of serial killers wearing horrific masks or carrying chainsaws; this is so far from the truth and all it does is take away from us the reality that we may well be standing next to a serial killer in the grocery store queue – he doesn't look like a killer so he can't be a killer. A serial killer is a true master at hiding his emotions, allowing him or her to blend seamlessly into society. Their victims fall for the lure, never seeing that they could be in the grip of a serial killer. Once the victim has been reeled in, the fake persona goes and the real killer surfaces, many killing with whatever weapon they can find, while others take their victims to a place where they have planned the murder down to the last degree.

The Biggest Step

While it would not be fair to turn the aftermath of one of these murders into something trivial, the true controversy amongst the serial killer theorists lies in the how and the why; how does a person go from fantasy to killer and why? Every one of us has individual genes that determine our personalities; they define who we are and what we are. There is one common belief that it is these genes that cause a person to become a serial killer but, as we have already seen, these killers are not born; they are made.

In the year 2000, Dr. Richard Davidson from the University of Wisconsin produced a report with the results of brain scans done on more than 500 people. The scans were split between those considered normal and those prone to violence. The study determined that the images, of those who had antisocial or aggressive disorders and were convicted of murder, showed activity in their brains that were different to those who were normal. If the findings from this study are correct then it could suggest that murderers are born not made. They must have had a completely different makeup genetically than those who are not violent. The scans showed that there was a relationship between the amygdala, which controls violent and negative emotion, the anterior cingulate cortex, which controls how we respond to conflict, and the orbital frontal cortex, responsible for controlling and restraining emotional outburst on impulse. The research showed that, on the violent subjects, there was little activity in the frontal cortex and the cingulate cortex but in the amygdala, the activity was the same or higher than it normally is. However, two people exposed to the same circumstances in their childhood and the same cultures will not necessarily both go on to become serial killers so, while research is useful in showing us what is going on in the brains of violent people, it doesn't necessarily follow that they were born that way.

Beyond the Pleasure Principle

In 1920, Freud published a book called Beyond the Pleasure Principle and, in it, he hypothesized that violence and aggression revolve around two instincts – the life instinct and the death instinct. When people have experienced an event that was traumatic for them, they will often re-enact this experience. According to Freud, people do this because they have an unconscious wish to die. The death instinct gives people negative energy that they use to create self-destructive behaviors. Sometimes the energy gets directed outwards instead of inwards and is then expressed through violence or aggression.

The life instinct, on the other hand, is when people attempt to make life better for themselves and to create goals to work towards. Freud maintains that people who are born with the death instinct go on to commit terrible crimes against people even though they know what they are doing is not right. Let's take Jeffrey Dahmer as an example again. Before he committed any murder, he got drunk because, deep down inside, his conscience was telling him that he was doing wrong.

Although Freud is not wrong in his theory that destructive behavior tends to be repeated, only a small fraction of serial killers actually falls into this category. Although we know that a serial killer commits a terrible crime repeatedly, it isn't always an unpleasant experience for them. Dahmer was 18 when he first killed and it was after that he started drinking because his conscience told him what he did wasn't right. Although he knew that, he continued with his killing spree because it gave him pleasure to commit horrific acts of violence on other human beings.

Genetic Differences

Every one of us has the same classification – we are all human. But that doesn't mean we are identical in genetic makeup. Each one of us is unique – you only have to compare fingerprints or skin tone of any two individuals to see that we are not the same. Genetics, like beauty, isn't only skin deep though. It goes much further, affecting our entire system including our thoughts and our minds. Back in 1915, Freud said that it is the active stimuli in us that make us act the way we do. In his words, those stimuli are "emanating within the organism and penetrating to the mind". If that really is true then that says that we, as humans, do not have any control over our own actions and that we are born with the active stimuli – these are what determine when we take flight or when we take action. Many argue that genes are the key to understanding the mind of a serial killer and that the only way we can stop them from committing their first murder and kick-starting a terrible spree is to find the defects in their genes early in life.

Again, we all have a different makeup but there are proponents of the thought that DNA differences do not have anything to do with whether a person becomes a serial killer or not. Indeed, most psychologists and criminologists do not focus their attention on genes, rather they study the childhood of the killer, their surroundings, and their origins.

When Jeffrey Dahmer was a child, he was an active, happy child. His father said that he used to love playing with other children, he was outgoing, happy and fun to be with. Do these sound like the characteristics a serial killer would show if he was born with aggressive genes? So, what changed with Dahmer? According to research, it all changed when his father got his Chemistry Ph.D. and moved the family to Ohio. They moved three times before they settled in Bath and at that point, Dahmer's parents noticed that he had gone from being an outgoing fun-loving child to an antisocial and shy one. The next step was when he began to pick up road kill and dissect it during experiments.

Psychologists in social behavior and criminologists constantly argue that it is bad experiences and "repeated psychological trauma" in childhood that lead to a child carrying out aggressive and harmful acts, such as killing animals. In Dahmer's case when his parents got into a fight, he would disappear into the woods, feeling lonely, and sit with a pile of dead animals he had found. He felt abandoned, not just by his parents, but by his classmates and he attempted to draw attention to himself by acting up and doing things that were not classed as socially acceptable. In his mind, the dead animals gave him the emotional release and the comfort that his family and friends couldn't.

Arnold Arluke is a criminal psychologist and he looked at the criminal records of more than 100 animal abusers and compared them to the same number of criminal records for those who didn't abuse animals. His findings showed that those who abused animals were more than 5 times likely to go on to commit rape, assault and eventually murder. What came out of this study is that many serial killers would be animal abusers in their childhood because they had no power against their parents and other adults who had control over them. With the animals, especially small animals, they felt that they had the control and power to dominate them and to do exactly what they wanted with them.

Childhood Rejection

Eric Hickey, an eminent criminologist, carried out a study on 62 serial killers, all male. He determined that 48% of them were rejected in their childhood by their parents or another adult who was important to them. Although this happens every day, all over the world, it does provide a representation that this could be a turning point in those that do go on to become serial killers. For some children, rejection pushes them into self-indulgence and they are not able to determine their own identity as they go through puberty. It is the significant experiences in childhood that turn people into violent criminals, not the trivial ones.

Serial killers who were the victims of rejection and/or abuse, turn to fantasies for comfort and dreams that take them to places where they are in control. They take these fantasies and they make them into a reality and live the dreams they have. Jeffrey Dahmer felt that he had been rejected by both parents and, because of this, he never revealed his violent thoughts about homosexuals. Instead, these thoughts stayed deep inside of him and he began to have fantasies about homosexual relationships. Only his fantasies went further; instead of just having sex with a man, he fantasized about killing him afterward. The need or desire to kill strongly fulfill a sexual desire in killers who manifest their fantasies into a reality that they have control of. Because they did not have a proper family relationship, they do not have a real understanding of how to interact and coexist in peace with others. That leads to another common conception about serial killers – they are violent and there is only one way to stop them; end domestic violence in their household.

One of the most important things we can do to stop serial killers from being made is to fully understand why they do it, not just how. So-called hard evidence was found by scientists who claim that genetics is the key in determining who will go on to become a serial killer. This goes against what the psychologists and criminologists claim, in that it is events such as abuse and abandonment at vulnerable times in childhood that create the foundation and the setting that grows the serial killer.

Both arguments have some founding and both have, to a certain extent, been proven through years of research but neither one, on its own, answers the question – why do serial killers exist? In truth, the answer lies in a combination of genetics and upbringing. Not all children who are abandoned or abused go on to become serial killers – if they did, the world would be severely decimated in terms of population. It is true that many victims of abuse go on to become violent themselves when they are adults but, in order to go from that to being a serial killer, it comes down to biochemical makeup.

So, nature or nurture? Which is it? Nature certainly does play a large part in who we are, the traits that we are born with but, in most cases, those traits do not become exposed unless there is a mechanism in place to expose them. Unless there is a balanced combination of natural defects in terms of genetics and the nurturing that they are brought up in, a violent person is not likely to go on to become a violent serial killer.

Do you like this Book?

Then please leave a review on Amazon for me!

Go to this URL to leave a review: http://amzn.to/2xifUMc

Chapter 3: Psychological Phases of a Serial Killer

Back in 1988, a psychologist by the name of Joel Norris determined and described a number of psychological phases that a serial killer goes through. Norris had worked extensively for the defense teams of a small number of serial killers from Georgia, all convicted of their crimes, and had also carried out more than 500 interviews with convicted killers in his bid to determine exactly what phases a serial killer goes through, from start to finish.

The Aura Phase

The very first phase that Norris determined was called the Aura phase. During this time, the killer begins to withdraw from reality and his senses begin to heighten. This can be anything from a few moments to a few months before the killing and it may even start out as a fantasy, which the killer could have been experiencing for some time. The killer attempts to make himself feel better about things through drugs or alcohol.

The Trolling Phase

The next phase is known as the Trolling phase and this is where the patterns of behavior that the killer uses in identifying and stalking his victim are defined. Ted Bundy, for example, would put his arm up in a sling and then ask his victims for help carrying books or some other package, to try to get them into his car. Some of his intended victims were lucky enough to escape and they all said the same thing – up to the moment that they were attacked, Bundy was in complete control of himself.

The Wooing, Capture and Murder Phases

The wooing phase is the period of time that a killer takes to win over his victims before he lures them into his trap. In the capture phase, the killer may render his victims helpless with something like a blow to the head or lock them into a room or vehicle. This is the moment that the killer savors. The murder phase is very often a ritual, an enactment of a disastrous experience the killer lived through as a child but with the roles reversed.

The Totem Phase

Once the killer has made his kill, he will sink into depression and, to preserve the success of the murder, many killers will develop a kind of ritual to help them. This is why you often hear of killers who fill books or walls with press clippings or with photographs of their victim. Some keep trophies in the form of something that belonged to the victim or even a part of their body. Some killers will consume a part of their victim's body, some will craft clothing out of their victim's skin or reveal a body part from a victim to a later victim. This kind of trophy keeping is designed to retain the image of power that the killer experienced when he killed.

The Depression Phase

This is the last phase. Now dead, the victim doesn't represent what the killer thought he or she would and the fantasy of that individual, the one that tortured the killer, remains. There is no satisfaction at the end because in the eyes and the mind of the serial killer the fantasy that caused so much tension has not yet been fulfilled. Because of this many serial killers get depressed and will soon start to fantasize about new violent ways to fulfill their fantasy. In every murder he commits after the first one he will try to make the crime scene equal to his fantasy and because the killer doesn't have any sense of self, he may even confess his crimes to the police before the fantasy starts up again. However, the victims are not real people to a killer and any recollections that the killer may have are likely to be somewhat vague, as though he were watching another person commit the crime.

Chapter 4: A Glimpse Inside the Mind of a Serial Killer

One eminent doctor, Helen Morrison, has interviewed around 80 serial killers across the world. Dr. Morrison is aiming to identify exactly what causes a serial killer to take that path in life and how they develop. To that end, she has even acquired a piece of the brain of one of the worst serial killers, John Wayne Gacy. Here are some of the findings that Morrison has made from years of research, findings that allow us to get a glimpse inside the mind of a serial killer:

No Empathy

Perhaps one of the most difficult things to grasp is how a baby can develop into becoming a serial killer. In the very early stages, a baby will quite happily be passed from one person to another but there is a certain point at which the baby will develop attachments and, as such, will become very upset when they are removed from their primary caregiver or from the person that they have formed that attachment with.

This attachment is the first indication or awareness to a baby that it is a separate person who is dependent on others for their needs. Serial killers will not develop that awareness or feeling and will never really see themselves as a part of the world. It is partly because of this lack of awareness that, although there are several ways that a serial killer will hunt in, most will never develop any kind of attachment to their victims emotionally. Take a man who loses his temper, jealous of his wife looking at another man. He may kill his wife because of that jealousy. A serial killer, on the other hand, will not have that emotional attachment to a victim. There is no appreciation, no awareness of the emotions that the victim demonstrates, such as terror, fear, and agony. All the serial killer sees is an object, not even a living human being. They have no feelings and no real motives for their murders; they kill just to kill.

Experimentation

Because the serial killer will never become attached to a victim, they are able to carry out experiments on the people they kill. Take Robert Berdella, for example. He is better known as the Kansas City Butcher, responsible for raping, torturing and then murdering at least 6 male victims between 1984 and 1987. He also experimented on each victim and kept notebooks on him or her. One part of his experiment involved pouring Drano (a drain cleaner product) down their throats so that they were not able to scream. This could be seen as being synonymous with a child who pulls the wings off a fly, just to see what happens.

John Wayne Gacy, another famous serial killer, also carried out experiments on victims and showed not one ounce of emotion while he did it. According to Dr. Morrison, the fact that there is no humanity at all is "more than just being psychopathic", simply because a psychopath is able to express emotions.

Lack of self-control

Many serial killers describe their killings as an addiction and that killing gives them pleasure. To continue to get this pleasure the addiction needs to be fed, hence why the serial killer continues to kill, in many cases, for long periods of time. The serial killers can in other words not control themselves enough to withstand the urge to keep murdering people. Dennis Radar or the "Btk killer" (you will read more about him in chapter 6) is a good example of this. Radar has described how he had an addiction. An addiction he could not control. This lack of self-control made him do terrible things, terrible things that a person with regular self-controlling abilities, would never do.

Power

The idea of power seems to be a commonality when it comes to serial killers. Many have described that they got a feeling of power when killing and doing other horrendous things to their victims. When they are in control of the victim they derive satisfaction. This is one reason why some serial killers keep their victims alive for some time, performing different kinds of torture on them and so on.

Chromosomal Abnormalities

If a potential killer has a chromosomal abnormality, it will begin to become apparent during puberty. Serial killers tend to be men, and they begin to develop and display homicidal tendencies when the abnormality begins to express itself. There is no single gene identity but the sheer fact that most of the world's serial killers are or have been men leads us to believe that changes in the male chromosome makeup could be a trigger. Right now, research on how and why the gene changes are ongoing but most serial killers will make their first kill during those early puberty years.

Clueless Partners

While Dr. Morrison was carrying out her research, she also managed to interview the wives of some of the serial killers. From what she found out, not one of the women were consciously aware of what their husbands were doing. Or, at the very least, they never asked any questions about it. John Wayne Gacy buried all his victims beneath his own house but, when Morrison asked Gacy's wife, Carol Huff, if she ever smelled anything odd, she said that her husband had explained it away as mice. And she never challenged that, accepting his explanation completely. That said, although the women may be aware on a subconscious level that something is not right, not only will they never question it, they will never get involved in the actual murders.

This has nothing to do with equal opportunities. As I said earlier, most serial killers turn out to be men and, while there may occasionally be a female companion, they are rarely responsible for initiating the crimes. It is rare for a serial killer to have a female companion; they prefer to work alone. The partners or wives of the serial killers tend to be somewhat incomplete themselves, which makes it very easy for the killer to draw them into their lives and under their spells – these that hold down a relationship, that is. If there is something missing in the woman, the killer will usually be able to fulfill it and most of the women are extremely passive with no assertiveness at all. However, this is incomplete research because, very often, the wives or partners will not speak to reporters, doctors, or researchers without the express permission of their partners, something that is very rarely given.

Difficult to Spot

You may find it difficult to understand how a woman could not be aware that her husband is a murderer, especially when the bodies are being buried beneath your house. However, it is not that easy to spot a serial killer because they won't show you anything that will give the game away. They can be extremely charming people, the man next door, not a screaming knife-wielding psychopath. It is because they act so ordinary that they can lure their victims in.

Just the Beginning

Right now, the research into serial killers is still very much in its infancy and the governments are not overly receptive to the research just yet. In fact, Dr. Morrison must get permission from the government of any country that a serial killer is incarcerated in to interview them. In fact, there is a landmark case that dates to 1973, Kaimowitz vs. Michigan, that decrees prisoners are not allowed to take part in any research because they are not capable of any free will.

This is a culture that prevails the world over and this means that researchers like Dr. Morrison find themselves stuck. Much of what they can say about the brains of serial killers is speculation based on what they already know about the human brain. Dr. Morrison has been luckier than most and has been able to interview a large number of serial killers but, because the world has become desensitized, governments are often very difficult to convince to allow the research.

Chapter 5: 5 Different Serial Killer Personalities

A real life serial killer is not a fictional super villain and they are not so easy to spot because they live their lives without raising any suspicion. Take Ted Bundy, Harold Shipman and Fred and Rose West, for example; these managed to give off an air of normality, while beneath the surface bubbled something very sinister.

To help us to understand the different types of serial killers which may, in turn, help us to understand more about what goes on in their minds, Dr. Elizabeth Yardley, the director of the Center for Applied Criminology, based at Birmingham City university, has gotten together with experts working at Real Crime magazine to help uncover the characteristics that may show us what a real serial killer looks like and what makes them tick.

Power Junkies

Many serial killers exhibit an affinity with power, even when they have been arrested and can kill no more. They display an intentness on exerting control over those around them and will very often hold back on snippets of important information as a way of keeping control and power over a situation, asserting what is, in essence, a very warped sense of authority.

Example: In the 1960's, Myra Hindley and Ian Brady were convicted of the murders of 5 children and, to this day, Ian Brady has refused to give up the whereabouts of one of their victims, Keith Bennett.

Expert Manipulators

Time and time again, serial killers have used the need to please and a sense of vulnerability very effectively to hide their true personalities. Some of the most famous serial killers in the world have exhibited a very frightening ability to manipulate everybody around them, pressing all the right buttons so that they are presented in a false light. Many serial killers also manipulate situations so that the blame is passed on for their actions. They may even use hot issues or psychological research to explain away their actions.

Example: Dr. Harold Shipman was a respected doctor and used that position to gain the trust of his victims.

Braggers

The egotistical nature of some serial killers means that they can't help themselves and have to brag about what they have done, whether it is aimed at themselves, at law enforcement, an accomplice or even the next victim. Example: Moors murderers Ian Brady and Myra Hindley would often go back to Saddleworth Moor, where they buried their victims. They would take trophy photographs of the desolation of the landscape as a way of reminding themselves of their heinous crimes. It was these photos that helped in their conviction and helped police to locate three of the bodies that were found on Saddleworth Moor.

Superficial Charmers

Serial killers exhibit a very strong grasp of the emotions of other people and they may be very quick at picking up on weakness or a vulnerability that they can exploit, charming the person into doing something they wouldn't normally consider. They will be able to tempt other people to their side and gain charge over a situation by using common sense and compliments.

Example: Jeffrey Dahmer, otherwise known as the Milwaukee Cannibal, was responsible for the murders of 17 boys and men between 1978 and 1991. Using superficial charms and compliments, he was able to lure every victim into his house where he murdered them.

Average Joes

This may well be the scariest of them all because these serial killers look like real pillars of the community when you first see them. However, this is just their way of getting people to trust them before they abuse that trust in the most horrendous ways possible. It is this tactic that has allowed many serial killers to carry out deviant practices behind the safety of closed doors.

Example: John Wayne Gacy was known as the Killer Clown. He was active politically in the Chicago suburb where he lived and did a lot of work for his local community, even performing as Pogo the Clown and events and parties. Behind closed doors, he raped teenage boys, murdering them, and then burying them under his house.

Chapter 6: 10 World Famous Serial Killers

We all know what a serial killer is, just by watching one of the numerous crime shows on television or reading one of the hundreds of crime books. Some of these may be fictional but the subject is far from made-up; indeed, they offer us a glimpse into the reality of the serial killer. In order to better understand the serial killer and what they are capable of, I have listed below 10 of the very worst serial killers in history:

1. Giles De Rais

Born in 1404 in France, French nobleman Giles De Rais was a decorated captain in Joan of Arc's army. After leaving he turned to torture, rape, and murder, with all of his hundreds of victims being young children, mainly boys. He had a morbid fascination with the suffering and pain of each victim and used inhumane methods of torture before murdering them. During the 1440's De Rais was tried and convicted of sodomy, heresy, and murder. His punishment, carried out to the letter, was hanging and then burning his body to a pile of ash.

2. Andrei Chikatilo

Andre Chikatilo was born in 1936 in the Ukraine. Other names that he has been known by are the Red Ripper, Butcher of Rostov and the Rostov Ripper. His first murder was committed on December 21, 1978, a 9-year-old girl by the name of Lena Zakotnova. He attempted to rape her but, as the child was struggling, he cut her with a knife, ejaculating as he did so. Most of his victims were young children and he would rape and murder them before mutilating them. He had even been known to consume some of the body parts. He was arrested in 1980 and confessed to 56 victims. On February 14, 1994, he was executed with a bullet to the head.

3. Colin Ireland

Colin Ireland, otherwise known as the Gay Slayer, was born in Dartford, Kent in England in March 1954. His decision to kill only gay men was made because he saw them as easy targets and he decided that nobody would be bothered if they died or disappeared. Over the course of 4 months, he murdered 5 gay men and would call the police constantly to ridicule them for not catching him. In December 1993, Ireland was jailed for the 5 murders, receiving one life sentence for each one.

4. Dennis Radar

Dennis Radar was born in Pittsburg, Kansas in 1945. He was known as BTK, which stood for his methods – blind, torture, kill. He murdered 10 people around Wichita in Kansas, sending the police letters to claim each death, providing proof with an item he would take from the victim or a photo of the victim themselves. All the murders took place between 1974 and 1991 and, after a quiet period of 13 years, his letters reappeared. Radar was arrested in 2005 and sentenced to one life sentence for each of the 10 lives he took. During the trial and during interviews Radar has said that he was driven by pleasure and compulsiveness. He describes how his impulses controlled him and that he had an addiction, which he could not control. An addiction making him create fantasies about killing people, fantasies he later carried out in real life.

5. Dr. Harold Shipman

Born in Nottingham, England in 1946, Dr. Shipman, otherwise known as Dr. Death, became a real blot on the landscape of English medical history. In 1999, he was arrested for more than 200 murders, all of them his patients and mostly elderly women. There was no violence or sexual attack and there is no known reason for any of the murders. He has been sentenced to 15 consecutive life sentences.

6. Gary Ridgeway

Gary Ridgeway was born in Salt Lake City in 1949 and was otherwise known as the Green River Killer. He is, without a doubt, the absolute best proof of deception. Married three times, Ridgeway was very social. None of his wives ever suspected or ever thought that he could be responsible for the murders of more than 49 women, most likely much more. His victims were mainly runaway teens and prostitutes and took place over a period of about 20 years. He was arrested in 2001 and found guilty, receiving a sentence of 48 consecutive life sentences with no parole.

7. Javed Iqbal

Born in Pakistan in 1956, Iqbal was also known by the name of Kukri and has confessed to murdering more than 100 runaway and orphan boys over a period of 18 months. He would drug his victims and then rape them, strangle them, and chop their bodies into pieces. Those body parts were liquefied in a vat of hydrochloric acid and then disposed of in a nearby river. He has allegedly claimed he has no regrets and he kept a photograph of each victim, along with other details written in a diary. He and another accomplice were sentenced to death in 2001 but both were found strangled to the death with the sheets from their prison beds.

8. Jeffrey Dahmer

Jeffrey Dahmer is perhaps one of the better-known serial killers. He was born in May 1960 in Wisconsin and earned himself the name of the Milwaukee Monster. He was responsible for the murder of at least 17 men and boys between 1978 and 1991, killing his first one when he was just 18 years old. In 1991 he was arrested when a victim got away and flagged down a passing police car. Police found bodies in vats of acid and heads stored in Dahmer's refrigerator. He was charged with multiple counts of necrophilia, sodomy, and cannibalism and was sentenced to 15 consecutive life sentences. He never served his time because he was beaten to death by another inmate called Christopher Scarver.

9. Dennis Nilsson

Dennis Nilsson was born in Scotland in 1945 and was otherwise known as the Muswell Hill Murderer. He murdered more than 15 boys and men after luring them into his home. After murdering the bodies, he would preserve them and sleep with them in his bed. As he lived alone and was very much a loner, he claimed this was to make him feel better. He would never have been arrested but for the plumber who came to unblock the drain. He found pieces of body flesh blocking up the drain and reported them.

It turned out that, when the bodies began to decay, Nilsson would chop the body up and then drain it. In 1983, he was sentenced to life in prison for all the murders.

10.   Ted Bundy

Ted Bundy was born in 1946 in Burlington, Vermont. He had several different aliases but his real name was Theodore Robert Cowell. He is another of the most famous serial killers in the world and lured his victims in by gaining their trust. He would rape and then strangle his victims, disposing of the bodies near to Taylor Mountain where he would then visit with the bodies, lying with them and, on occasion, having sex with the decomposing corpses. He confessed to murdering 30 young women between 1974 and 1978 but it is believed that the number is much higher. Bundy, being an intelligent man acted as his own attorney during his trial and was able to cross-examine all the prosecution witnesses. He also, once imprisoned, assisted the police with the Green River Killer case in order to provide insight into how the mind of a serial killer works. On January 24, 1989, he spoke his last words, "I'd like you to give my love to my family and friends" before he was executed.

Conclusion

I want to thank you for reading my book, I hope that you found it interesting. My aim was not to have you spend your life trying to determine if every person you meet or see is a potential serial killer. What I wanted to do, and what I hope I managed to achieve, was to give you a glimpse inside the mind of a serial killer, a brief look at who these people are and what turns them into serial killers.

As you have learned from reading this book, there are many factors that could determine why a person becomes a serial killer. It's pretty clear that serial killers are made not born. Although genetics certainly does play a part. Some people will be born with certain traits making them more likely to react poorly to certain types of experiences, in this case, some kind of abuse during childhood. A combination of natural defects and a bad upbringing, making the child lack empathy and creating a need for the feeling of power. Is probably the biggest determining factor why some grow up to be cold-blooded killers. In addition to this, a lack of self-control and an addiction to the pleasure received from killing seems to be other important factors.

If we look at the common traits that I went through in the first chapter of this book. There are many traits that can be linked to a lack of control and a feeling of powerlessness. Some examples are Psychological abuse, sexual abuse, unfair punishments, and bullying. This together with many serial killers describing the power they felt when acting out their crimes makes me believe that the aspect of power is very important when it comes to serial killers and should be further investigated.

All serial killers, without exception, commit the most horrendous and violent of crimes against humanity. They think nothing of their victims and will do whatever they want to their victims so they can fulfill their own needs. No matter what the reason behind the crimes of any serial killer, it is important that we understand what makes them turn to serial killing in the first place. Only then can we hope to identify the potential of a person who takes this route in life and, perhaps, take the steps needed to lead them down a different path. There is still a lot to be learned about serial killers but I hope that this book has given you some knowledge about them and a glimpse inside their minds.

It must be said, before I go, that not everyone who exhibits the traits discussed in this book will go on to become a serial killer, far from it. In fact, only 1% of the total number of murders committed across the world is the work of a serial killer.

Once again, thank you for reading my book if I may ask a small favor of you? Would you please take a few minutes and **leave a review** for me at **Amazon.com**? Go to this URL to leave a review http://amzn.to/2xifUMc **Thank you.**

53586993R10031

Made in the USA
Middletown, DE
28 November 2017